I0820670

A Day in the Life of a Green Sea Turtle

Julie Murray

Abdo Kids Junior
is an Imprint of Abdo Kids
abdobooks.com

Abdo
A DAY IN THE LIFE
OF AN ANIMAL
Kids

abdobooks.com

Published by Abdo Kids, a division of ABDO, P.O. Box 398166, Minneapolis, Minnesota 55439.

Printed in the United States of America, North Mankato, Minnesota.

102025

012026

Photo Credits: Getty Images, Shutterstock

Production Contributors: Teddy Borth, Jennie Forsberg, Grace Hansen

Design Contributors: Candice Keimig, Pakou Moua

Library of Congress Control Number: 2025936503

Publisher's Cataloging-in-Publication Data

Names: Murray, Julie, author.

Title: A day in the life of a green sea turtle / by Julie Murray

Description: Minneapolis, Minnesota : Abdo Kids, 2026 | Series: A day in the life of an animal | Includes online resources and index.

Identifiers: ISBN 9798384907299 (lib. bdg.) | ISBN 9798384907992 (ebook) | ISBN 9798384908340 (read-to-me ebook)

Subjects: LCSH: Green sea turtle--Juvenile literature. | Sea turtles--Juvenile literature. | Marine reptiles—Juvenile literature. | Reptiles--Behavior--Juvenile literature. | Animal behavior--Juvenile literature. | Herpetology--Juvenile literature.

Classification: DDC 597.92--dc23

Table of Contents

A Green Sea Turtle's Day

It is **dawn**. The green sea turtle starts its day.

It was sleeping safely in the **reef**. It is ready to come out.

The green sea turtle swims to the surface. It takes a breath.

It floats in the water. The sun warms its body.

It spends the morning feeding.

At midday, it rests on the **seabed**.

In the afternoon, the green sea turtle eats some more.

It swims to a cleaning station.

Fish clean its body.

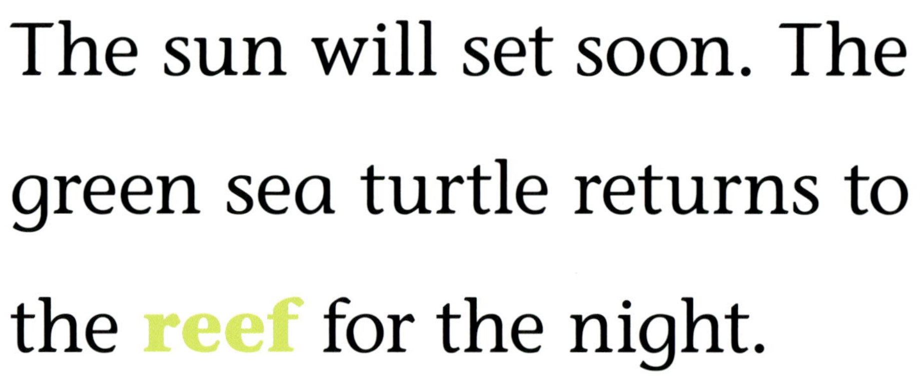

The sun will set soon. The green sea turtle returns to the **reef** for the night.

Green Sea Turtle Facts

Can live for 80 years or more in the wild

A female lays her eggs on the same beach she hatched on

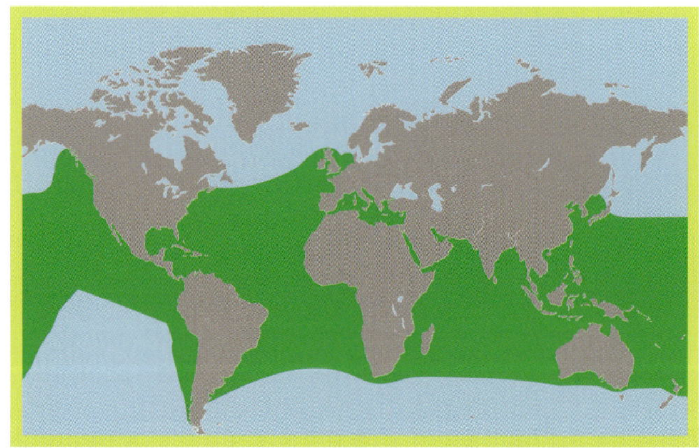

Lives in warmer ocean waters throughout the world

Can weigh up to 700 pounds (317 kg)

Glossary

dawn
the first daylight that appears in the morning.

reef
a ridge of rock, sand, or coral at or near the surface of ocean waters.

seabed
the floor of an ocean or sea.

Index